SLAPPIN':
A COMPLETE STUDY OF
SLAP TECHNIQUE FOR BASS

by
Marc D. Ensign

Audio Contents

Online Audio & Video

Audio
www.melbay.com/96534MEB
Video
dv.melbay.com/96534
You Tube
www.melbay.com/96534V

1 2 3 4 5 6 7 8 9 0

Visit us on the Web at http://www.melbay.com — E-mail us at email@melbay.com

Marc D. Ensign

A Berklee College of Music graduate, Marc D. Ensign currently resides in the New York Metropolitan area where he teaches, plays sessions, Broadway shows, and club dates.

Dedicated to the memory of Ron Ross
(June 27, 1954 - July 20, 1996).
You are an inspiration to us all.
Go Forth, Ron!

Special thanks to my parents for their undying love, support and faith.

Marc D. Ensign can be reached via E-mail at mdensign@aol.com or visit http://members.aol.com/MarcEnsign/main.htm.

Recording performed by:
Marc D. Ensign: Electric Bass
Eric Panyan: Drums

Photography by Sal Trombino

Recorded at Fox Studio's in Rutherford, New Jersey
Engineered by Dave Blake
Assisted by David Paolazzi and Mike Santasiero

Table of Contents

Introduction

So, you want to learn how to play slap bass, huh? Whether you are into funk, R&B, fusion, jazz, rock, punk, reggae, alternative, or any other style, I welcome you to the world of slapping! With this book I have compiled a number of exercises, grooves and examples written over years of teaching, playing, and most importantly, listening to different players and styles of music. This book is aimed to benefit all levels of players, from beginner to advanced. I strongly feel that everyone has something to gain from each one of these lessons.

I am probably going to mention this about two thousand times in the course of this book, but I can't impress upon you enough the importance of what I am about to say. Take every single technique, exercise, groove, and example very slowly. The varied techniques and ideas presented, when applied correctly, will prove to be invaluable to you, but you must remember to proceed at your own comfortable pace. Do not continue to the next lesson until you have successfully completed the current one. When I say "successfully completed" I mean that you should be able to play each example at a moderate tempo, repeating it at least three times in a row without stopping or making any mistakes.

Next, I am only going to mention this once...right now. Whether or not this slap style is a new technique, chances are you will be using muscles and motions in both your hands and arms that are unfamiliar to you. Do not try to be a hero. You may get blisters on your fingers or the muscles in your arms may get sore. I cannot impress upon you enough that if this gets painful for whatever reason take a break, stop practicing, relax, make sure that your positioning and technique are correct. Most importantly, DO NOT PUSH YOURSELF. Tendonitis could be right around the corner. We are in no rush to learn this stuff and there is nothing wrong with taking a breather every now and then.

In the back of this book you will find a discography that is basically a list of albums and bass players that represent the use of this technique. It would be my suggestion to pick up a couple of these albums whether or not you recognize the names of the groups or styles. Remember, in music it is very important to keep an open mind to all styles of music. You would be surprised what a rock bass player can learn from a jazz player and vice versa.

If you have access to a metronome, it would be a wise idea to use it. By using a metronome, you are forcing yourself to play these examples in time and at a slow tempo. The recording that accompanies this book contains all of the examples and grooves to insure that you are getting the correct sound and using the techniques accurately, and it gives you the opportunity to play along with them.

All right, all right, enough lecturing – it's time to do some damage.

Notation Key

Before we actually begin there are a couple of things you should know. Here are just some technical terms that will be used throughout the course of this book.

For starters, from this point on you will no longer have a pinkie, ring, middle or index finger. The fingers on both hands will be numbered as follows with the exception of your thumb which will be called...your thumb (pretty clever, huh?).

Index - **1st finger**

Middle - **2nd finger**

Ring - **3rd finger**

Pinkie - **4th finger**

Next there are a number of symbols that will be placed above the notes that concern the technique which you will be using.

T - Thumb Slap	**P** - Pop	**H** - Hammer-On	**O** - Pull-Off
X - Ghost Note	**L** - Left-Hand Slap	**S** - Slide	**TR** - Trill

Occasionally you may see the symbol **TS** or **PS**. This means to attack the string with either your thumb (T) or pop (P) and then slide (S) it up to its destination note.

The first track of the audio contains all four open strings to be used for tuning purposes. The **drums** have been panned to the **left** and the **bass** is panned to the **right** so when practicing these exercises you will have the opportunity to isolate either instrument, or keep it in the middle to hear how the two interact together.

For those adventurous types out there who want to try to read the music rather than the tablature, here is a quick idea of how the notes are laid out on the staff.

Lines: 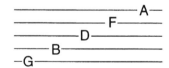   Spaces: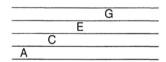

Finally, if you have never seen tablature before, here is a quick and easy explanation. Each of the four lines on the staff below represents a string. The bottom line is the low E string, up to the top line which is the high G string. The numbers on those lines all represent the fret that you should be playing on the given string. This example would be 1st fret E string, 3rd fret A string, 5th fret D string and 7th fret G string.

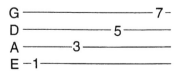

Lesson 1a: Thumb Technique

The most important aspects of slapping is the basic thumb and pop techniques. It is crucial to really understand and perfect the motion, sound and feel of these two techniques before continuing on through the book. The purpose of these exercises is to gain the accuracy necessary in playing this style of music. Although these exercises may seem exceptionally easy, be sure to work on them at a slow and comfortable pace, concentrating on every note. Try to perfect the tone of each one as you strike it. This chapter is the backbone of slap bass playing, and the more proficient you are, the easier the rest the book will be.

The first technique we will be concentrating on is the thumb slap. The key to this technique is the twisting motion in your wrist, but be sure NOT to swing your arm. Your wrist should be perfectly straight, and should not bend at any time when playing this. Stick your thumb out as if you were hitchhiking and curl your fingers (Fig. 1). When you strike the strings, you want to hit them between the last three frets of your bass with the bone right on the joint of your thumb (Fig. 2). Twist your arm to allow your thumb to hit the desired string and bounce off as soon as you have made contact. This gives it a whipping-type motion and allows the string to ring out. If you are not getting any sound, chances are you are probably not bouncing off the string quickly enough. Be sure to relax your hand, and don't feel as though you have to hit the string very hard.

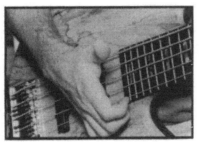

Fig.1

Fig.2

Example 1: Track 2

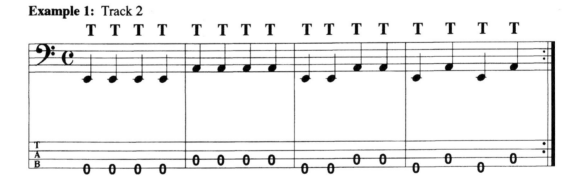

Example 2: Track 3

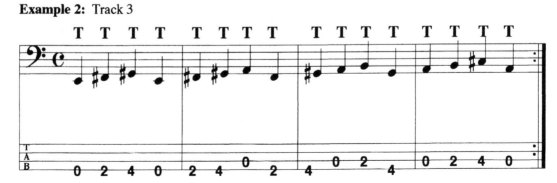

Lesson 1b: Pop Technique

The next technique that we will be using is the pop technique. This, along with the thumb, will give you the basic slap bass sound that you are used to hearing.

In this technique, you are going to use either the first or second finger on your right hand to pop the string. There is a valid argument why either finger could be used. I prefer to use my second finger because it is longer, and as we get more advanced we will get into using both at the same time for slapping chords and other techniques. Your second finger will then be at the target note, so it is important that you are able to use it strongly. That does not in any way mean that using your first finger is wrong – the most important thing is that you are comfortable with whichever finger you decide to use.

OK, now the same rules apply when working on this technique: play it slow, perfect it, and only then should you move on to the next section of this lesson. First take your finger and curl it underneath the G string and pull it away from the bass (Fig. 1). Next, let the string go and you should hear a strong snapping sound when the string hits the frets. Now try it on the D string.

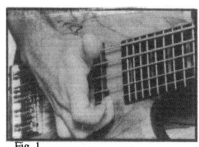
Fig. 1

Example 1: Track 4

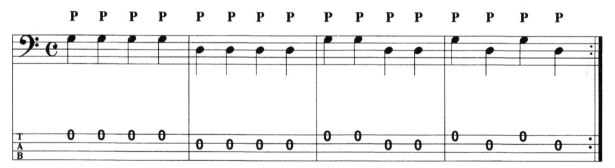

Example 2: Track 5

7

Lesson 1c: Exercises Combining Basic Slap and Pop Technique

Now remember, the most important thing about these exercises is the technique; be sure to take all of them slowly. Do not continue to the next lesson or exercise until you feel as though you have perfected the one you are currently on.

Example 1: Track 6

Example 2: Track 7

Example 3: Track 8

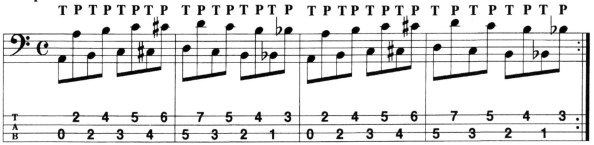

Example 4: Track 9

Lesson 1d: Grooves Using Basic Slap and Pop Technique

Be sure to watch out for the rhythms. This is where things start to get tricky.

Example 1: Track 10

Example 2: Track 11

Example 3: Track 12

Example 4: Track 13

Lesson 2a: Hammer-On Exercises

A hammer-on is a series of two different notes tied together, where the first note is the lower of the two. You begin by articulating the first note, using the notated right-hand technique. The second is articulated only with your left hand by forcefully pressing the string down on the proper fret.

To do this, hold the first note with the first finger of your left hand (Fig. 1) and strike that note using the given right-hand technique. Without attacking the next note with your right hand, you strongly press the string down on that fret, using the second or third finger on your left hand (Fig. 2).

Fig. 1

Fig. 2

Example 1: Track 14

Example 2: Track 15

Example 3: Track 16

Lesson 2b: Pull-Off Exercises

Pull-offs are very similar to hammer-ons, only this time the first note you strike will actually be the higher of the two notes. Before playing either note, the first finger on your left hand should already be prepared by pressing down the fret of the second note (Fig. 1). After striking the first note, you are going to lightly roll the finger of your left hand off the string in a plucking-type motion (Fig. 2), allowing the second note to ring through.

Once mastered along with hammer-ons, these techniques will add greatly to your playing and give the illusion of playing much faster and smoother lines.

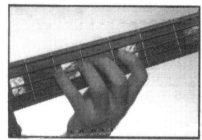
Fig.1

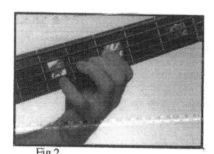
Fig.2

Example 1: Track 17

Example 2: Track 18

Example 3: Track 19

Lesson 2c: Grooves Using Hammer-Ons and Pull-Offs

OK, as we are getting into more complicated things, it means now, more than ever, you should be taking these exercises and grooves very slowly. Once you feel comfortable enough with each one at various tempos, you should then go on to the next one.

Example 1: Track 20

Example 2: Track 21

Example 3: Track 22

Example 4: Track 23

Lesson 3a: Ghost Note Exercises

Ghost notes play a huge part in the rhythmic and percussive sound of slap bass playing. Since they have no audible or distinguishable tone, a ghost note is described as a "click" or percussive sound used to enhance the rhythmic feel of a groove.

To play a ghost note, you attack the string with your right hand the way you normally would using a thumb slap or pop. With your left hand you lightly mute the given string by touching it hard enough to dampen the note, but not so hard as to have the string touch the fret giving the note an actual pitch.

Ghost notes are notated by using an "X" placed on the staff corresponding to the string on which it would be played. For example, a ghost note slapped on the "E" string would be notated on the first ledger line below the staff, or in tablature, it would be on the bottom line indicating the "E" string – this goes for all four strings.

Example 1: Track 24

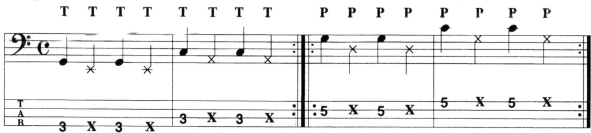

Example 2: Track 25

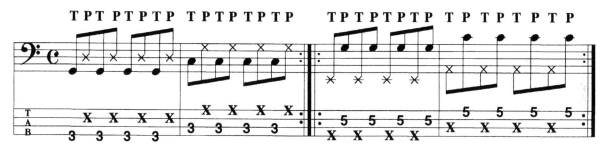

Example 3: Track 26

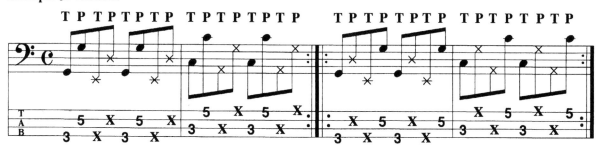

13

Lesson 3b: Ghost Note Grooves

Now remember to take each example at a slow tempo until it feels comfortable enough to speed up. (I told you I would say it two thousand times.)

Example 1: Track 27

Example 2: Track 28

Example 3: Track 29

Example 4: Track 30

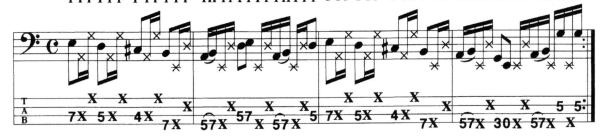

Lesson 4a: Left-Hand Slap Exercises

Now, where would we be without left-hand slap?!?! The left-hand slap is very similar to ghost notes in the sense that it is one of those techniques that does not seem to make much of an impression, but without it the groove sounds very empty. It adds a certain percussive flavor to what you are playing and aids in the muting of open strings and other ringing notes. By giving your right hand a little break, it also makes you sound like you're playing a lot faster than you actually are...pretty cool, huh?

Take your 2nd, 3rd, and 4th fingers of your left hand off of the neck. Keep your thumb anchored on the back and leave your 1st finger there to mute the strings and hold down the fret of the note to be played previous to the left hand (Fig. 1). Swing your fingers down onto the strings, but don't bounce them off because you want it to sound like a ghost note (Fig. 2). At no time during this technique should your right hand be doing anything (except maybe signing autographs to all those people that you just impressed).

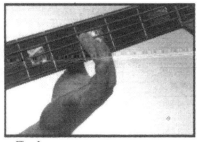
Fig. 1

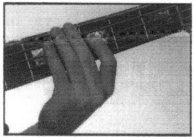
Fig. 2

This technique is also going to be notated differently. First of all, above the note will be the "L" symbol indicating the left-hand slap technique. The note itself will be an "X," similar to a ghost note. Just so we do not confuse the two, the left-hand slap note will be placed on the space provided for the "E" on the staff, and between the "A" and "D" lines on the tablature.

Example 1: Track 31

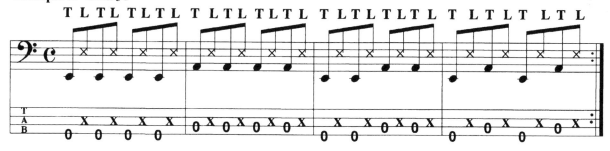

Example 2: Track 32

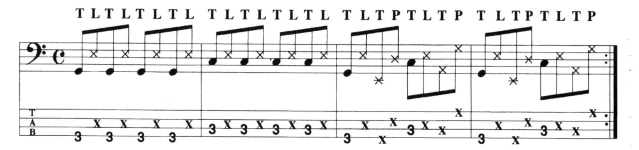

15

Lesson 4b: Grooves Using Left-Hand Slap Techniques

Example 1: Track 33

Example 2: Track 34

Example 3: Track 35

Example 4: Track 36

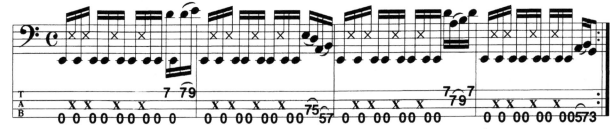

Lesson 5a: Open String Hammer-On Exercises

Remember the hammer-on exercises we worked on way back in Lesson 2?!?! Well, open string hammer-ons are identical – only now the first note you will be attacking is an open string... hence the name "open string hammer-ons." More often than not the note you will be hammering on to after the open string will be played with your first finger.

Example 1: Track 37

Example 2: Track 38

Example 3: Track 39

Example 4: Track 40

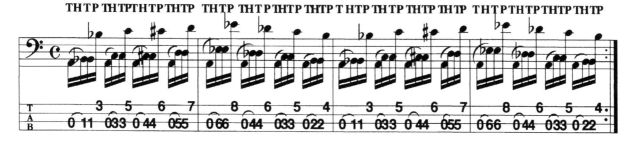

Lesson 5b: Grooves Using Open String Hammer-Ons

Example 1: Track 41

Example 2: Track 42

Example 3: Track 43

Example 4: Track 44

Lesson 5c: Open String Pop Exercises

Yet another technique that is just what it sounds like. (Gee, this music thing is easy, isn't it?... that was a joke). Popping open strings is a neat technique because open strings tend to ring more, giving the groove a fuller sound and filling up any empty space. When played correctly, open string pops can really add a lot to a groove or lick without sounding too busy. Be sure when doing this that the fingers on your left hand are arched over all of the strings so you don't dampen the open string that is ringing.

Example 1: Track 45

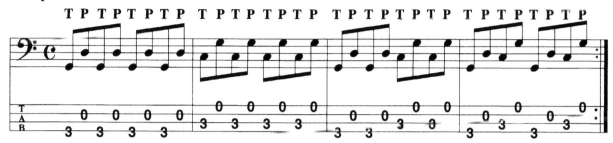

Example 2: Track 46

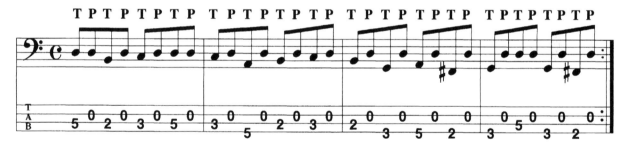

Example 3: Track 47

Lesson 5d: Grooves Using Open String Pops

Example 1: Track 48

Example 2: Track 49

Example 3: Track 50

Example 4: Track 51

Lesson 6a: Double Slap Exercises

We haven't really gotten too fancy when it comes to using our thumb up until now...the Double Slap Technique. The double slap consists of quickly slapping the string twice with your thumb giving the groove more drive when used correctly. (Be sure not to overuse this technique...that can be really dangerous.) To do this you just slap as you normally would the first time, but as soon as you bounce off the string you want to quickly snap your thumb back, repeating this technique. At first it might seem a bit awkward, but once you practice it enough times you will realize that it is really just one motion rather than two.

Example 1: Track 52

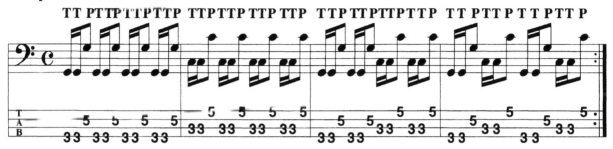

Example 2: Track 53

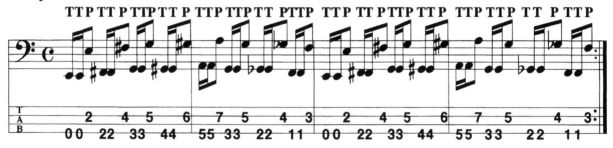

Example 3: Track 54

Example 4: Track 55

Lesson 6b: Grooves Using the Double Slap Technique

Example 1: Track 56

Example 2: Track 57

Example 3: Track 58

Example 4: Track 59

Lesson 7a: Double Stops and Other Chords

Although bass is not necessarily known for its use as a chordal instrument, that doesn't mean that you can't occasionally play them. When playing more than one note at a time it is always good to play those notes higher up on the neck so they don't sound so muddy because of the low frequency of the bass. For the most part, because you will be playing these notes on the D and G strings, you are going to either pop them or slide up to them.

This brings us to the technique of popping with two fingers...see I told you we would get to it. The way you are going to do this is to pop the lower of the two notes with your first finger and the higher with your second finger, regardless of which finger you have been popping with up to this point. Curl your fingers underneath the appropriate strings and pull them using the same technique as you would for popping just one string (Fig. 1). Most importantly, when you let them go make sure that both notes snap and ring out at the same time. If you have to slide up to the notes, you will be slapping the first note somewhere in the middle of the neck and sliding it up until you reach the destination note. Once you reach that note, you will then pop the second one while the first is still ringing.

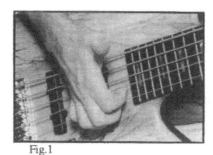
Fig.1

Example 1: Track 60

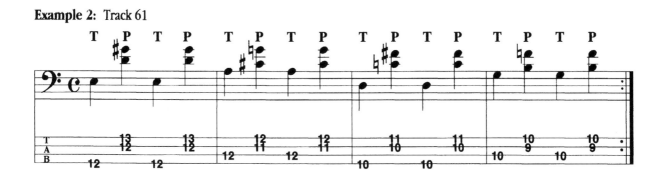

Example 2: Track 61

Lesson 7b: Grooves Using Double Stops and Other Chords

Example 1: Track 62

Example 2: Track 63

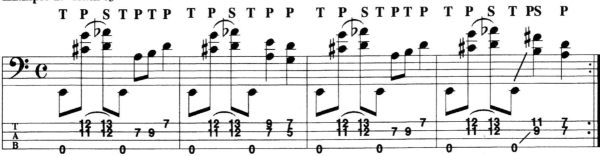

Example 3: Track 64

Example 4: Track 65

Lesson 8a: Double Pop Exercises

I saved this one for last because as far as I am concerned this is the hardest and by far the coolest technique that I know of. It is very similar to the technique we used for the double stops, only this time we are going to make the notes snap and ring out separately.

What you want to do is anchor your first and second fingers of your right hand on the appropriate strings (Fig. 1) just as you did for the double stops. Rather than pulling the strings out and making them snap at the same time, you are going to roll off away from your bass using a twisting motion in your wrist (Fig. 2). This motion is very similar to the twisting of your wrist when slapping, only now you will be doing it in the opposite direction. Be sure to keep your right-hand fingers firm and do not pull the strings. Let your fingers make the strings snap as you roll them off (Fig. 3).

  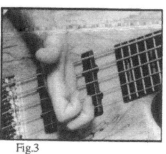

Fig.1　　　　　　　　Fig.2　　　　　　　　Fig.3

Example 1: Track 66

Example 2: Track 67

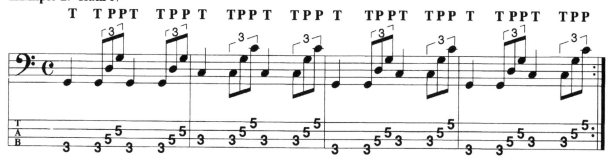

Lesson 8b: Grooves Using the Double Pop Technique

Example 1: Track 68

Example 2: Track 69

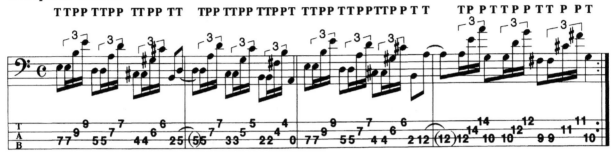

Example 3: Track 70

Example 4: Track 71

Lesson 9: Other Licks and Tricks

I realize that I haven't shown you everything there is to know about slap bass playing, and the fact is that neither I nor anyone else will be able to do so. Sometimes you just need to discover things on your own, and by introducing you to some other new techniques, I am leaving the door open for you to experiment even further on your own.

I decided that rather than adding each of these tricks as a new chapter, I am going to lump them all together in the same chapter and just explain them, and leave it up to you to further them by creating your own exercises and grooves. Let's face it, if you have successfully made it this far, you should have NO problem with this stuff. There is a possibility you may see some of these techniques thrown in Chapter 10, the advanced grooves section, so be sure to check them out.

Trills

A trill is an embellishment on a note, making what was once just a simple note "funkified"! All it really is is a series of fast hammer-ons and pull-offs usually a half-step away. Because a trill is played quickly and not necessarily in time, it has to be notated a special way:

This is how it will be notated:

This is how it will sound:

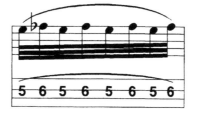

Octaves

Octaves are a pretty simple thing to play, right? Well, how about when you want to play two notes an octave away at the same time? The way you are going to position your right hand is to grab the lower note as if you were going to pick it (not slap it) with your thumb, and use your first or second finger to play the higher note as if you were going to pop it (Fig. 1). Now to play the notes all you have to do is bring your fingers together as if you were trying to pinch them, and you got it.

Fig.1

Double Thumbing

This is a really cool technique, but depending on how their right-hand positioning is, some people have a harder time with it than others, so don't get frustrated. What you want to do is slap the string with your thumb the way you normally do, but instead of bouncing off, follow through and snag the string with your thumb on your way back up (Fig. 2) giving the string another attack. This technique is very similar to the style in which guitarists use a pick.

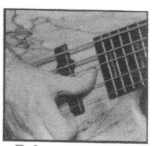

Fig.2

27

Lesson 10: Advanced Grooves and Solos Using All Techniques

So, you have made it to the final chapter. I congratulate you. At this point, if you have followed all of the instructions carefully, taken your time in learning each lesson and exercise, and perfected each technique, you must be a pretty dangerous player.

Now that you have all of these important tricks, licks, and techniques under your belt, there is one more thing I have to teach you...less is more. Now what I mean by this is that although you know all of this stuff, you have to learn how to properly use it, and how to properly not use it. No matter how technically awesome you are, your job is still as a bass player, and with that comes a lot of responsibility. There is a time for everything – sometimes you will have the opportunity to really shine, like on a bass solo, and other times you will just have to lay back and make someone else shine by playing just a simple groove. The only way to really learn this is through experience and by using your best judgment.

The next couple of pages are dedicated towards some advanced stuff such as funk solos and longer, more intense grooves. This final chapter is not so much the end of the book as it is an introduction into improvising and creating your own style. My goal in adding this chapter is to leave many doors open and give you new ideas to experiment with on your own. By taking some of the grooves that we worked on throughout this entire book and rearranging, combining, and alternating them you have started on the road to creating your own style.

Example 1: Track 72

Be careful, this is one of those new techniques I told you about. This groove contains the octave pops that we went over in the last chapter.

28

Lesson 10: Advanced Grooves and Solos Using All Techniques

This next example is a groove played over an A Blues progression. Watch the rhythms, slides and the chords that have been thrown in there. It might not be a bad idea to try and learn this groove in different keys. Try playing the same or similar groove over a G Blues, B♭ Blues, or E Blues. Now take just the blues progression and improvise your own line over it. Don't be afraid to experiment.

Example 2: Track 73

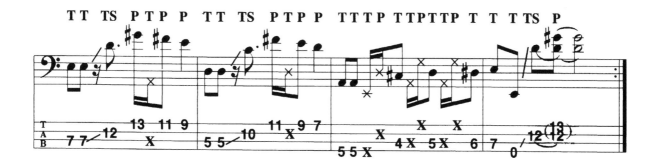

Lesson 10: Advanced Grooves and Solos Using All Techniques

Hold onto your hats folks, this is the tough one. This last example is an eight bar funk bass solo played over an E7 groove. Within this solo you'll notice that I used many of the techniques that we worked on throughout the book. Be sure to take this one very slowly, get the feel and the techniques together, and notice the structure of the solo itself and how it is built. Once you are able to play it well, try and alternate it a little by putting in your own licks and ideas here and there. Soon you'll notice that it sounds nothing like the original, and you have just created your own groove or solo.

Example 3: Track 74

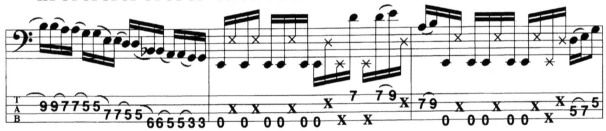

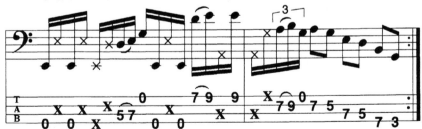

Discography

Probably the biggest problem with learning a style that is relatively new to you is not having the opportunity to hear it in context. The most important part of music is listening, so if you don't know what to listen to, what do you do? Well, have no fear, that is why I have come up with this short discography to give you a few ideas of where you can hear this style and these techniques being used. I realize that I have probably forgotten a bunch of players and albums, and I deeply apologize to each and every one of them, but there is so much good music out there I hardly have the time or the paper to write it all down. This list will give you a solid start in building your CD collection, and by doing that, you will also build your musical vocabulary through listening and transcribing some of the parts played by these incredible players.

Jazz/Funk/Fusion

Marcus Miller
David Sanborn - "Straight to the Heart"
Marcus Miller - "The Sun Don't Lie"
Miles Davis - "Tutu"

Stanley Clark
"If This Bass Could Only Talk"
"School Days"

Victor Wooten
Bela Fleck and the Flecktones - "Bela Fleck and the Flecktones"
Bela Fleck and the Flecktones - "Flight of the Cosmic Hippo"
Bela Fleck and the Flecktones - "UFO TOFU"
Victor Wooten - "A Show of Hands"

Abraham Laboriel
"Dear Friends"
"Guidum"

Gary Grainger
John Scofield - "Pick Hits Live"
John Scofield - "Loud Jazz"

David LaRue
Dixie Dregs - "Bring 'em Back Alive"

R & B

Bootsy Collins
Bootsy Collins - "Back in the Day"

Marcus Miller
Luther Vandross - "Any Love"
Luther Vandross - "Give Me the Reason"

Larry Graham
Sly and the Family Stone - "Anthology"

Rodney "Skeet" Curtis
P-Funk All Stars Live

Stanley Clark
Animal Logic - "Animal Logic"
Animal Logic - "Animal Logic II"

Rock/Alternative/Metal/etc.

Flea
Red Hot Chili Peppers - "Red Hot Chili Peppers"
Red Hot Chili Peppers - "Freaky Styley"
Red Hot Chili Peppers - "Uplift Mofo Party Plan"
Red Hot Chili Peppers - "Mothers Milk"
Red Hot Chili Peppers - "One Hot Minute"

Les Claypool
Primus - "Suck on This"
Primus - "Sailing the Seas of Cheese"

Mark King
Level 42 - "Level 42"
Level 42 - "World Machine"
Level 42 - "A Physical Presence"
Level 42 - "Running in the Family"

Made in the USA
San Bernardino, CA
28 August 2017